Activated Monologues
for Female Characters

ACTIVATED
MONOLOGUES
for Female Characters

edited by Kathryn Funkhouser

Published in 2026 by Stage Partners
PO Box 4795
Stamford, CT 06907
www.yourstagepartners.com

ISBN: 979-8-89099-264-2

Printed in the United States of America

10 9 8 7 6 5 4 3 2 1

Questions? Contact us at info@yourstagepartners.com

CONTENTS

COMEDIC MONOLOGUES

How to Use This Book

"Where's the action?" Any actor approaching a scene asks this question, and we found ourselves asking the same one as we approached the idea of a monologue book. We didn't particularly yearn to publish *The Big Book of People Speaking in Long Paragraphs*. We wanted to create a tool that actors could actively use as they craft a monologue for an audition, class, or performance. The action we aim to take at Stage Partners is always to connect theatre artists with the work of our playwrights—the best resource we can offer. Their plays are filled with great roles to inhabit and characters with surprising things to say. It's up to you to activate them in performance. We hope this book will help get you started along the way.

That's also why we are organizing these volumes by the gender of the characters speaking, rather than the actors that might play them. We're here to offer you the characters the playwrights have crafted, roles to play—and we welcome any actor to explore the roles as written. Note that although all of the characters in this volume *can be* portrayed as female, we've also included some roles that the playwrights have designated as flexible too, so not all of them *need* to be female.

Ready for action? Here's what to look for:

An active verb in bold is included in each monologue's introductory description. How many times have we heard our acting teachers say it? Find the verbs! That's why the introduction to each monologue includes not only an overview of the character and the context of their monologue in the play, but also an active verb. This is a jumping-off point, a place to start in your portrayal—there are always more verbs to find!

★ Meet prompts provide information about the character written by the playwright elsewhere in the play.

✗ **Play** prompts suggest exercises and ways to play with the portrayal of the character to inform your performance.

⚡ **Note** prompts include casting notes and production notes that are relevant to your monologue.

📖 **Discover** prompts suggest further reading: more plays you can read by the author, more places to find similar monologues, and other resources you can explore to inform your understanding of the monologue.

🔓 **Unlock** prompts are exercises that you can try for any monologue in this book. Trying to crack your monologue, but getting stuck? These are questions to ask yourself to get your character moving, with rules you can adjust to your class or your personal process. There are no right or wrong answers as long as they resonate with you.

READ THE PLAY: Finally, because all of the plays in this book are Stage Partners plays, **every monologue includes access to read the entire play that the monologue is from online for free.** At the end of each monologue, the **READ THE PLAY** section will include information about the play with a QR code and web address for the play's profile page. If you create a free account on the Stage Partners site, you can click the "Read for Free" button on the upper right-hand corner of any play profile page to read the entire script.

Remember, as you work on any monologue, if you find yourself coming up blank, you can always go back to the text and read the full script of the play to find a spark of inspiration.

Now, we've got one last action to give you:

GO!

—Kathryn Funkhouser, Editor

DRAMATIC
MONOLOGUES

THOSE WHO REMAIN TURN THE PAGES
Del Martin

*In a dark and frightening time, a community meets to decide the fate of a prisoner they call "the monster," whom some hold responsible for all of their troubles. If the group votes "Yea," the prisoner will be set free; "Nay" means the prisoner will die. Here, Terra **implores** the community to consider the prisoner's humanity and their own.*

TERRA

I…I planned on coming up here and saying to you that I think you're all good people. But that would have been a lie. No group of people is all good. I'm not even sure I know what goodness is. We're here. We're alive, which means we've done things. Things we're not proud of, and, yes, some things we are. There's no point in lying to you all. No one here is all good…but at one point we were. In each of our lives there was a point in time when we were innocent. Some of you may not remember it, or believe you ever were so pure… And some of you operate under the delusion that you still are…good…and righteous… and worthy… To those of you who are so certain of your own virtue I offer you nothing. You're not listening to me anyway. Nor am I speaking to those who are convinced of their own wickedness, who revel in it. You've wandered so far from the path, you've convinced yourselves there never was one… No… I am speaking now to those who know their souls are blemished, and hope to some day wash them clean. You wear your imperfections not with pride, but with humility. It is to your humility that I appeal now.

We are gathered here to make a decision. We hold in our hands a life. And you may tell yourselves that it is a monster, a demon, something evil that has come from afar. Each of you, I'm sure, would shoot a rabid dog if it meant protecting your family. You'd do it without hesitation, and you would do it without the need of a committee. The very fact we're here should indicate something... This is no dog. This is no demon. This is a person. And I am not here to tell you that this is an innocent person. I'm not here to claim they are pure and true. No...I am not here to convince you of their current innocence. But I do believe that like you...and me...and everyone, they once were...

There is something rotten in this town. I have no doubt of this. But I do not believe the accused brought it here. And yes, there are witnesses, and some of those witnesses are people I call my friends. And, in fact, I believe them... Insomuch as that I do not believe they are lying...I simply believe they are mistaken. I know the accused. I know she is troubled...

I know that she has caused trouble... But is she a monster? Is she the cause of all of the suffering and sadness this town has seen? I wish she were. I wish it were only that simple. But it is true that what this town decides tonight could very well decide our fate. If we do this thing. If we kill this so-called "monster," we damn ourselves. There is but one life in danger tonight, but make no mistake, there are many souls that are in peril. So I ask you...take your page and mark "Yea." Not to save the life of a monster, but to save yourselves.

- **Discover** more monologues in the full script of *Those Who Remain Turn the Pages*, as different members of the community testify in the trial that threads together the different parts of this piece.

- **Meet** Terra, in the playwright's stage direction: *"(She takes a breath before speaking to the crowd. She doesn't love talking to a crowd, but she is also someone who will do what needs to be done.)"*

☞ **Unlock** monologues by asking: Who is your character talking to? A crowd? An individual? If they are talking to multiple people, are there moments where they might speak to someone specific?

If they address the audience, who is the audience to them within the world of the play? For example, in *Those Who Remain Turn the Pages*, the audience is included as part of the community voting on the prisoner's fate.

What does your character want from the people they are talking to? How do they hope or fear the people they are talking to will react?

If your character is speaking to another individual, what is their relationship? What history do they have? Does the relationship change over the course of the monologue?

READ THE PLAY, a full-length horror drama for 8–25 actors:

yourstagepartners.com/those-who-remain-turn-the-pages

There are zombies outside, but two cousins trapped in an abandoned restaurant find the other humans sharing their hiding place might be even more dangerous. A group of friends meet in secret about whether it's time to flee their hometown being slowly overtaken by a vampire-like population...unless it's already too late. *Those Who Remain Turn the Pages* is a terrifying and timely triptych of tales that makes life-or-death decisions inescapable for its characters and its audience alike—because when darkness falls, people start to show you who they really are.

This full-length play contains the one-act plays Those Who Remain *and* Turn, *each of which may be performed and licensed as individual one-acts, or as part of the complete full-length play.*

THE GIRL WHO WAS A HUNDRED GIRLS
Finegan Kruckemeyer

Eight months after her sister Suse was kidnapped outside a local mall where they were shopping together, Mel **bares** *the many layers of her grief as she struggles to find a way to get through each day.*

MEL

At first you're shocked, and the shock is an uncomfortable thing. It itches and catches on your clothes. You see it out of the corner of your eye and find yourself pausing mid-conversation. The shock has silenced you.

After a while, you mourn, you wail. Your parents wail too, so the wailing becomes a conversation. If one wails more than you, you become silent—you go to them. If you walk past a bedroom, and there sits a father and he is looking at a photo. And then you walk past the same room two hours later, and he is looking at the photo still, then you must make a choice.

You choose to close the door.

After more time, you become angry. You cut your hair, which is one of the fundamental actions of grieving. Other fundamental actions are damaging photos, biting your nails, hating the people around you who can't understand. You won't always feel this way—toward those people, or your photos, or your nails. But for now you can. It's your entitlement.

Your school grades improve. People don't expect this—they expect the opposite. But fuck them for expecting. They haven't lost a sister. You become a wonderful student. You hand in work early. You smirk at teachers who try to understand "what this might mean."

And then the pivotal moment. You are making toast. You put in the bread and it cooks for two minutes, which is perfect, just the way you like it. And you remember that it used to be every time you put in bread, you had to change the setting to two minutes, because it was on five. Because your sister, who was kidnapped, who has not been heard of since, she liked her toast dark.

And it is toast—it is toast that makes you collapse. Your mother finds you. You hold each other like you haven't before. Your dad comes home. He enters the kitchen and sees you both and gets onto the ground and holds you. And together you cry and you cry and you cry—warm, wonderful tears that make no apologies, that are shared between the only three who understand.

And your grades return to normal after that. You let your friends in again after that. You get a part-time job. You get a cat. You forgive yourself a bit.

And then one day it's suddenly been eight months and you go to the mall after school, and cross at the lights, and cough into a hanky, and notice a broken sign outside the deli, and walk in and feel the eyes of everyone on you, and don't care, because you've got good at that. And then as you're looking at a dress, you recognize the shadow on the ground beside you.

And you smile and turn, too quickly, too confidently, because you know it's your sister standing there, and she's about to flick your arm like she always does. And you come face to face with…

A stranger. Of course it's a stranger, because your sister was kidnapped eight months ago.

And everything you've done over that time that has got you to this point, where you feel like maybe life has more possibilities than just grief—all of that disappears. And suddenly it's like the first day, all over again.

📖 **Discover** more monologues for the many female characters who are connected across time in the full script of *The Girl Who Was a Hundred Girls.*

🪶 **Note:** The playwright's stage direction offers options: *"(She may be walking to work, or the monologue may be delivered in another way.)"* What are some different actions you might try in conjunction with Mel's words?

↤ **Unlock** monologues by finding the shifts and turns. Where *exactly* in the monologue does your character shift? What changes for her physically, vocally, tonally? What exactly incites eachs shift in the moment? Is it somethings she sees, hears, learns, remembers?

Try imagining the thing that incites each shift for your character in as much detail as possible. Then, play around with imagining it the opposite to see what you find. For example, if a frightening animal approaches, what if it was beautiful? What if someone tells you good news and it was devastating somehow? What changes? Could it be both?

READ THE PLAY, a full-length drama for 7–18 actors:

yourstagepartners.com/the-girl-who-was-a-hundred-girls

Since her kidnapping, Susannah has been kept in a room where she sees no one but her own shadow on the wall. To bring her solace, her shadow offers her stories of other young women who seek the strength to face the impossible in different times and places: a bullfighting ring, a treacherous mountainside, a local service station. But when a whisper through the wall suddenly brings Susannah a connection to hold onto, a surprising connection also begins to emerge between the women's stories. Could it truly be possible for a story to set Susannah free? A breathtaking drama filled with resilience and hope.

QUEENS
Kristen Doherty

In this historical drama, King Henry VIII has discovered his fifth wife's relationship with another man, Thomas Culpeper. Now, awaiting execution in the Tower of London, the former queen Kathryn Howard **fortifies** *herself to face death as best she can.*

KATHRYN HOWARD

If I look outside, I can still see them, though darkness spreads its blackened fingers to extinguish the day, I can still see them… Oh my love. My Thomas, is it you I spy? The very same face that would smile upon me with such love and affection…the very same face with eyes I could feel myself getting lost in… *(Haunted:)* The very same face that greeted me as I was brought through Traitors' Gate. Oh Thomas, I can't bear to see your face, once beautiful and serene, now distorted with fear and pain. Eyes piteously seeking me, and yet your head remains struck atop yonder pole, within my eyesight. Oh, take it away, take them away! For there beside my love is my traitor, Deneham… Eyes accusing, blaming me, blaming me, blaming me… Body gone, gore dripping… Don't stare at me! Stop looking at me!

(Sinks to ground:) Oh, oh, oh, I am so cold, so cold. Will I ever be warm again? However shall I overcome these last torturous hours before my life is snuffed out forever? Before I lose my precious head… *(She touches her head, her face tenderly:)* These eyes that looked upon you with too much love. These silly little ears that listened to the sweetness of your voice. These lips which kissed with too much passion, I say goodbye to you. *(She cries, then corrects herself.)* No, no, no… I must be well remembered. I must die with dignity, not with shame. I must be remembered in

my death as I never shall be in my life, with courage and decorum. Yes, I must do this right.

Lead me to the block, I must prepare. Then I am ready.

(She steps forward.)

I will remember those who have gone before me. I must be brave, and I shall remember them… *(She kneels and hesitantly puts her neck upon block, then recoils.)* Oh God! I smell blood. *(Panics, stands up and paces around crying.)* Oh God. I can't do this; I can't do this. I don't want to die; I don't want to die. *(A beat.)* …But what do I have to live for? Oh, Thomas, I will miss you forever *(A beat.)* …Or will I? Maybe I shall hold you in my arms once again… *(Composes herself.)* Oh Thomas, I never longed so much for anything, as I do to see you and to speak with you, which I trust shall be shortly now. That which doth comfort me very much when I think on it. Pray God, it is quick… Now I am ready.

📖 **Discover** additional monologues throughout *Queens* for many of the women in Henry's past—and one from a future he will never see.

READ THE PLAY, a full-length historical drama for 10–35 actors:

yourstagepartners.com/queens

King Henry VIII is trapped in purgatory, bound to his throne by a sinister Fool and the ghostly Women in White. Here in his gilded cage, he is forced to relive the sins he committed against his queens, mistresses, and people of the court, over and over again, for an eternity.

A one-act version of this play is also available.

ANTIGONE: 3021
Nina Mansfield

In this futuristic retelling of the Greek tragedy, Ismene's sister Antigone has been arrested for burying their brother, the rebel Polyneices, in defiance of Chancellor Creah's law. Alone in her bedroom, speaking to her online followers, conflicted Ismene **debates** *the morality of the situation.*

ISMENE

Hi. It's me. Ismene. And this is my vlog, *Ismene: Just Thinking Out Loud.* I know it's been a while since I've uploaded content. Those of you who keep up with current events—and I usually don't, but then I realized, like maybe I should because there's been a lot going on in Thebes. And as usual, my messed-up family is at the center of it all.

So here's why I'm back. I feel like I need to do something. This whole Antigone thing has gotten me so messed up in the head. She's my sister, and like, I keep thinking maybe I should have helped her, or worked harder to stop her. And you have to believe me when I say I would have stopped her if I could've, but now, I don't even know if that would've been the right thing to do.

OK, the truth is, and this is really hard for me to admit to, but I don't totally disagree with Chancellor Creah's law. I mean, yes, on a deep level I do. But there's a part of me that thinks, she's the leader now. She knows what to do.

And, I mean, I guess Poly was a traitor. People were saying he wanted to destroy our way of life. But he didn't actually want to deactivate the public cloud—he wanted to improve content. And all that stuff about the Oracle, he seriously just wanted the Oracle fact-checked—because, I mean, some say she'd been off on so much lately. And when they say he wanted to take away people's kids, I mean, that's like totally taking something he said once about learning pods out of context. But still, he did attack the city. And all the people who were against him, could they be wrong?

But Creah's law...I mean...we bury our dead in Thebes. We've always done that.

I figured my aunt wasn't actually going to have Antigone arrested. Okay, maybe arrested, but not executed. That was just politics. Those were just words, right?

But maybe we should start believing what comes out of people's mouths. You know, it's weird, that moment, you realize someone you thought you could trust, someone you had so much faith in, isn't who you thought they were. It's sort of this cold, empty feeling. It's like, how did I ever believe in this person. And you start to doubt yourself. You start to doubt everything. Reality. That's really scary. And that's kind of where I'm at right now.

So what do I do now? If you're watching this, leave a comment. Because, I know what to think. I just don't know what to do.

And don't forget to follow and like.

READ THE PLAY, a full-length dystopian drama based on a classic Greek tragedy, for 14–29 actors:

yourstagepartners.com/antigone-3021

It's the year 3021 and Thebes has just been through a bloody civil war. Chancellor Creah has decreed that anyone who buries the body of the traitor Polyneices will face death, but Antigone is determined to bury her brother, no matter the penalty. She brazenly breaks Creah's law and broadcasts her crime on the public cloud. Now Creah must decide if she will bend to the will of the people or punish Antigone for her crime.

A one-act version of this play is also available.

THE OLD WOMAN LOST AT SEA
Jason Lemire

Mildred sits at her unconscious friend Martha's bedside waiting for her to wake up, onboard the boat that has rescued them both. While Mildred took up the offer to come aboard the boat when a storm was approaching, Martha, suspicious of the ship's crew full of people who are "different," refused to leave her own rickety rowboat until her daughter rescued her from the water. Here, Mildred **beckons** *her friend to join her in a new world.*

MILDRED

That happens from time to time with these young ones. You know some of them haven't got the attention span for much. But it doesn't make me wish I was back in the ocean! It makes me wish you would wake up, so we could enjoy all this together.

   (A beat.)

Do you remember that time when we were playing cards. And we looked out the window. And saw that young man up on the roof of my neighbor's house? And he had a ladder. But he also had that white pickup truck. And it was an *old* white. That way how something that *used to be white* can be not quite white anymore, and it makes you think to yourself "uh-oh! This looks suspicious!"

Well, this young man, he had a truck just that color, and was up on my neighbor's roof and I happened to know that my neighbors were away. And do you remember? We started wondering, "what is this young man doing up on their roof?"

And he was far enough away that we couldn't exactly pick out what color *he* was. If you understand my meaning.

And just the evening before, on the news, they had an entire story on how they'll *pretend* to be working on a house, but really what they're doing is breaking inside, covering up your things with a work tarp, loading them into their truck, and just walking right off with everything. Right there in broad daylight. And no one says a word because it looks like they're supposed to be there.

And do you remember that that's what we thought *he* was doing?

Because, well goodness sakes, it had just been on the news!

So we called the police. And they said to keep an eye on him while they sent someone over. So we did. And that young man up on the roof, he kept on working. Hammering down the shingles. And we kept on watching.

Until we heard that patrol car pull up. And do you remember what we did? We shut the blinds. We did. Because we didn't want to see.

We did not want to see what they might do to him.

And I think that's when we knew. Deep down.

That we had made a terrible mistake.

(Mildred sighs.)

Being on this ship now, with all these people. These *young* people. These…*different* people.

It feels like a little bit of a second chance. If you understand my meaning.

I was thinking I might even run into that young man from the roof.

(A beat.)

I can't imagine what I'd say but…

(Mildred takes Martha's hand.)

I sure would like to say it with you.

↗ **Play** characters in contrast. Mildred's words to Martha become even more powerful when you learn more about Martha by reading the rest of the play. This monologue suggests they share a past, and begin in a similar place, but they make different choices. How is Mildred's arc different from Martha's? What makes her different from Martha as a person? What makes these two characters friends? What do they have in common?

⌐ **Unlock** monologues: If you're struggling to connect physical action to your character, try an unconnected one! Play around with simple actions that *don't* apply to the monologue or the play at all. How would your character deliver this monologue while making a sandwich? Exercising? Building with Legos? Maybe your character is a queen who would never make herself a sandwich, but you might find she'd assemble one with perfect efficiency, and think of ways to show efficiency in the way she moves her hand or takes a step. Need to get out of your head? Put different actions into an online randomizer, or on scraps of paper you pick out of a hat to try as you speak. If you're in a group, have a scene partner come up with an action to challenge you.

READ THE PLAY, a one-act drama for 8–11 actors:

yourstagepartners.com/the-old-woman-lost-at-sea

Take care of your own little boat, and let others take care of theirs. That's what Chelsea's mother Martha taught her as she grew up. But she also remembers the cost, and she can't look away when she sees someone drowning, like her mother can. When the seas turn stormy for Martha's own boat, she refuses to come aboard a bigger ship crewed by people different from herself—and they can only take so many of her cruel words. Is it too late for rescue? A lyrical one-act drama about empathy, inclusion, and charting a new course.

THE LITTLEFIELD GAZETTE DOES NOT END TODAY
Don Zolidis

*Over the course of their annual company picnic, the staff of the struggling local newspaper has been wondering about their future in the face of tough financial times and a changing media landscape. Here, the editor-in-chief, Trina, **confesses** the truth about the paper's future, and how much their work means to the community*

TRINA

This paper has been around for 126 years.

(Short pause.)

It's not going to make it to 127. I wasn't actually planning on talking about this tonight, but I heard a few people talking to each other and I think y'all deserve to know the truth. We have been doing everything we can. Gayle has been—I don't know when this woman sleeps. She has been fighting every minute of the day for us—same with everyone on the business side of things, Imani, Lamar, Rachel…they have been champs through this.

(Short pause.)

But there are some fights you can't win. And we ain't gonna win this one.

I don't know when our last issue is, we're figuring that out right now. But it's not gonna be long.

I love you all.

I love what you've done for this town.

There are so many scrapbooks filled with so many articles y'all have written—people cut 'em out, people save 'em, they put 'em on their fridges…you brought people together, you made people think, you told people the truth. Not everybody wanted to hear it, but everybody needed to hear it.

Y'all are my family. You need anything, you come find me. I'm not going anywhere.

Discover: While this monologue occurs near the climax of the play, other employees have their say in monologues throughout this ensemble piece before Trina breaks this news.

For more dramatic monologues by Don Zolidis, read his dramas *The Chips are Down* and *Monster.* Interested in the lighter side of his work? His comedies, such as *Haters* and *Princess Party Smackdown,* include monologues, and Vanna's monologue from *No Substitutes* is included in the comedic section of this book.

READ THE PLAY, a full-length dramedy for 10–18 actors:

yourstagepartners.com/the-littlefield-gazette-does-not-end-today

Something is different about the company picnic this year. After 126 years woven into the fabric of this small town, the Littlefield Gazette is closing its doors. For the staff, this is the last hurrah: the perfect time to tell a secret, confess feelings for someone, plan a new future.

What could they mean to each other now? And while we're at it, who brought the best pie? This rich ensemble collage of poignant, funny vignettes pays tribute to local news and explores what makes a community. 

NORTHVIEW HIGH SCHOOL WILL SHELTER YOU (IF WE MUST)
Emily Hageman

*After Darcy's brother committed a horrific school shooting at their high school, the remaining students have been sent to their rival school, Northview, to finish out the year. In this scene, Darcy has warily joined Northview students Jenny and Molly to work on a group project for class. After Jenny apologizes for previous thoughtless comments she made online, Molly tries to reach out to Darcy by expressing surprise that she's even attending school after what happened. In response, Darcy **unveils** how heavy her burden has really been.*

DARCY

Where else am I supposed to go?

> *(It could have been a sharp, angry question, but Darcy just sounds tired—so tired. It comes off sounding like an honest question. Where else can she go? Jenny and Molly say nothing.)*

I can't—I just wake up every day and I think—I can't do this. I can't be me. But I can't like…crawl out of my body and be someone else. I mean, I would give anything. Anything.

> *(A moment passes.)*

And I'm so—so angry. And I hate how angry I am, but I'm livid—and I'm—I'm ashamed. Like—more ashamed than I ever even remotely knew was possible. And I'm just like—looking at my life right now and everyone says that it wasn't my fault, but they say it so much that it makes me think—if they're trying so hard to convince me that it wasn't my fault, maybe it really was.

> *(A moment passes.)*

It's just—I can't do this. I can't. I don't want to—I don't want to do any of this. I mean, I would give up every good thing I've ever had in my life just to—to make all of this go away. Because—I don't know how I can ever live past this, I mean, this is just me now, isn't it? No matter how hard I try, this is going to follow me around for the rest of my life—it's going to hang over my head and I'm always going to know—how much I didn't know. But maybe I did know. And I'm so—I can't even explain with words just how…sorry. No. Forget it. This is—I don't know even know you, I'm sorry, I—

I'm not even—making sense.

I just…I can't explain…there's not enough words for me to say just like—how angry I am. And how much I—my mind is just scrambling twenty-four hours a day and I hate him and I am so hurt and angry and embarrassed and I don't even know how anyone can even look at me, but I get up every morning and I do all the stupid stuff that doesn't even matter and then I come to school and it's just…everything feels so small and hollow now. But I just keep doing it…because I don't know what else there is to do. I guess. I don't—understand. I don't—none of this makes any sense. And I'm not the kind of person who's like—you know, I don't believe that everything happens for a reason, but I do believe there's like—logic.

And cause and effect. And I—there's no cause, there's no effect, it's just like—staring into a black hole. And I just feel like…I'm inside of it. And he didn't kill me, but he did. But I didn't die. And he killed so many people. He killed them. How could—I've known him my whole life, how could he…he killed people. People with families and kids and friends and lives and—and I knew he was sick, but I didn't know…and even if it wasn't my fault, it must have been in some ways. It must have been. I don't know. I can't…I can't feel anything anymore. I don't want to feel anything ever again. I'm sorry. I'll…I'm sorry. This is—it's too much. It's way too much.

📖 **Discover:** Other students share their opinions in monologue form throughout this play—some funny, some dramatic. Mia's dramatic monologue from Emily Hageman's play *The Inexplicable Chaos Factor of Mia Gregory* is also included in this book.

🗨 **Meet** Darcy: In the Cast of Characters, the playwright describes Darcy as "broken, angry, strong."

READ THE PLAY, a full-length drama for 11 actors:

yourstagepartners.com/northview-high-school-will-shelter-you-if-we-must

In the aftermath of a horrific shooting at a neighboring high school, a group of students is asked to welcome their rivals into their school for the remainder of the year. Over FaceTime and Instagram Live, students from both schools struggle to navigate trauma and grief amidst group projects, student council meetings, and planning for prom. As their preconceptions about each other gradually begin to fade, surprising friendships begin to form, and everyone emerges transformed by the experience.

Written to be performed on stage or virtually.

This show can be cut into a shorter play by simply removing one or more of the scenes.

THE FULLEST
Min Kahng

After Emma watches a reenactment of her own life performed by her granddaughter Lily's college sketch comedy troupe, she has a heart-to-heart with Lily about her decision to discontinue dialysis. When Lily suggests that perhaps Emma is just tired and in need of encouragement, Emma firmly but kindly **guides** *Lily to understand her choice.*

EMMA

Now, hold on just a minute there, Lily. Sure, I'm tired. What person my age isn't? And sure I've been dealt crappy hands. What person hasn't? But I refuse to only view my life through the lens of the worst things that have happened to me. My choice to skip dialysis has nothing to do with giving up on life! I have lived a very full life, Lily. Abundantly full. I met my soulmate.

I have four children who are now adults and healthy and happy. And I was able to raise them right on my own, while still juggling a modest career. And I have seven grandkids, each so beautiful and unique. One of whom will be an amazing comedian and writer in the future. Do I wish I could see her do all the incredible things I know she'll do? Of course. And it breaks my heart that I might not be around for all your upcoming milestones. But I also know that spending hours hooked up to machines is not how I want to live the last years of my life. It's just my choice, my preference. Understand?

(Lily nods.)

Believe me, though, when I tell you that I am still going to live my life to the fullest even if my time is short. That's what God wants me to do. That's what I want to do. And that means I will be there for every comedy performance you have while I'm still here. And you can use my living room to rehearse any time. And I will be right here with a tray of cookies for your whole troupe.

I know it's scary to think about death, but I was always gonna die at some point. Knowing that it's sooner than later isn't particularly fun, but it does mean that the time I now spend with you or your mother or any person I encounter, whether it's going to routine doctor's appointments or hosting a re-telling of your own life story—this time is now all the more precious. And I love you, Lily. So much.

↗ **Play** with push and pull. Where does Emma push back against her granddaughter's assumptions, and where does she affirm and embrace her?

READ THE PLAY, a one-act dramedy for 8–20 actors:

yourstagepartners.com/the-fullest

A change in perspective can change your whole outlook—at least, that's what Lily's banking on when she surprises her grandmother Emma with a theatrical re-enactment of her life. Distraught by Emma's decision to forgo treatment for her terminal illness, Lily thinks her grandmother just needs encouragement not to give up, enlisting her community college sketch comedy troupe to remind Emma of her life's trials and triumphs so far. Only, Lily didn't exactly tell her friends what they would be doing, and she may not actually know everything about her grandmother's life. Maybe it's Lily who needs a new perspective on what it means to live life to *The Fullest* in this poignant, heartfelt dramedy.

Written as part of the California Thespians One-Act Play Commission, established by Stage Partners in conjunction with California Thespians.

FOUR FOUND A MOUNTAIN
Finegan Kruckemeyer

*After their parents' divorce, Lily and her brother Brian have moved to Mt. Cressy with their dad, and stumbled into a quest to restore the barren, crumbling town to life. As the siblings and two local kids haul a beehive up the mountain in a bathtub contraption, in hopes of finding flowers that used to grow in the valley, Lily **envisions** a new world that she shares with her mom in a letter.*

LILY

Through the thickest wilderness, we forged a path, Mom. We could hear the bees, thousands of them, as they wove through the shrub and foliage, and we pulled the hive after them. They had thoughts of pollen in their tiny minds and their wings beat excitedly against the dark Mt. Cressy air.

Behind us lay the town, and its empty streets, its crumbling shops, its fields full of weeds. Behind us lay a thousand people sleeping in their beds, not dreaming of the future, but remembering the past. They dreamt of days that held more and felt lighter. Dreamt of nights when friends would wander, laughing down the streets after the last ember of a bonfire had cooled, after the last sign from a street party had been taken down.

Into bed they once fell, Mom, smiling at the memory of neighbors visited, of songs sung, of laughter ringing in the crisp Mt. Cressy evening. But now they climb into bed only after checking every lock, after peering scared through every curtain. They pull the blankets to their chins and wait for morning to come. They wait for the day when the town can feel the sun rise properly again, when they can part their curtains, step onto their porches…and stretch their arms…

Eyes bright with the promise of a new day dawned.

📖 **Discover:** Finegan Kruckemeyer has many more great monologues for female characters in *The Girl Who Was a Hundred Girls.*

✎ **Play** with the clues you can gather from elsewhere in the play to discover why Lily she shares this moment with her mother in this particular way. Does the play explain why Lily is speaking to her mother in letter format, rather than over the phone or in person? Where is her mother, and why? Are there other letters in the play? If so, how is this one similar or different?

Now, you have more information that you can use to dive deeper. What might Lily be trying to communicate about herself when she describes this moment to her mother?

READ THE PLAY, a full-length adventure for young audiences for 4–11 actors:

yourstagepartners.com/four-found-a-mountain

When Lily and Brian's father moves their family of three back to the cozy little town where he grew up, they are surprised to find it quite different than he remembers. As times have gotten harder, the town itself and the connections between the people who live there have both fallen into disrepair. Yet there are new connections to make, and when Lily and Brian join forces with two new friends to find out the truth about a second moon that appears in the sky, a mysterious code, and a missing explorer, maybe there's hope for the future. An adventure for all ages about the power of young people to remind their community of what it once was and what it might become.

A one-act version of this play is also available.

#VIRAL
Maria McConville

*In this ensemble drama set at a modern-day high school, Megan **reckons** with her own culpability in a bullying incident, imagining what it will be like to run into her former target in the future.*

MEGAN

In five years I'll be home for Thanksgiving break.

I'll be in the check-out line at the grocery store.

My mom will be complaining that they didn't have the seasoning she wanted.

Or that it was too expensive.

The line will be long.

It's always long the day before a big holiday.

When we finally get there.

I'll look up in the cashier's face.

Through her long blonde hair.

Her bangs that cover her eyes.

And I'll see.

I'll see her.

And we will both look away.

We will both pretend we don't know.

That we used to

Have slumber parties

Study sessions

Family vacations

Clothing swaps.

We will both pretend the other doesn't exist.

It will be easier that way.

My mom won't notice either.

We'll pay for our groceries and head out into the frosty night.

But through the giant storefront windows,

I'll see her.

Fingers on the cash register keys.

And I'll spend a lot of time

In the next five years after that

And the next five years after that

And after that

Trying to forget.

The blonde girl in the store that night.

Who was almost as much of a stranger to me

As my sixteen-year-old self.

The girl who would do something so terrible.

And never look back.

 Discover more monologues in the full script of *#Viral* as well as in Maria McConville's play *#Censored.*

READ THE PLAY, a one-act drama for 7–40 actors:

yourstagepartners.com/viral-by-maria-mcconville

In this ensemble-driven drama featuring an all-female cast, five high school girls recount a cruel locker room bullying incident that is initially cloaked in secrecy, but ultimately goes viral online. What happens next forces the students to question their respective roles in the events that unfolded in that fateful day.

WRECKAGE
Peter Gil-Sheridan

*After her teenage daughter is terribly injured in an accident, Joyce speaks to her at her bedside. Unsure if she can be heard, she **bargains** with her daughter for a future together.*

JOYCE

I haven't always been your mother.

You don't really know all of me. I suppose I don't know all of you either, do I? Isn't it funny? Parents and children only know parts of one another. Of course, the parts you do know, you know really well. I bet you think I've never had an adventure. That I've never been terribly naughty, that I've always been a good girl. When I was seventeen years old, I spent half my high school day in beauty school. Now I'm not trying to give you any ideas, but do you know that I stole one of those heads you learn to cut hair on? I stole it because it looked just like me and when I wanted to climb out my window and down the maple tree, I would set up pillows and that head in my bed to look like I was sleeping there. I never got caught! Once I even came home and saw Mama talking to me...talking to me and I wasn't even there! I was just there laughing in a tree.

When this is all over, I want to get to know more of you. No sneaking. No lies. No omissions. We'll be best friends. Can I make you that deal?

⚲ **Discover** the many monologues spoken by characters throughout *Wreckage*.

✗ **Play:** To dive more deeply into the psychology of Joyce's character, you might study her powerful scene with Reverend Meyers later in the play.

↦ **Unlock** monologues with objectives. What does your character want when they speak their monologue? Objectives can be big (power) or small (a hamster), physical (food) or a deeper need (validation). Does your character have a single objective or multiple? How can you layer them? For example, if your character's objective is revenge, what if you also gave them the objective to take the ring off their enemy's finger?

Is each objective conscious or unconscious? What does your character think they want, and what do they really want? What happens if you layer a new unconscious objective under your conscious objective? For example, if your character's conscious objective is to steal someone's chapstick, try your monologue once with the unconscious objective to destroy their life, and once with the unconscious objective to marry them one day.

READ THE PLAY, a one-act ensemble drama for 11–20 actors:

yourstagepartners.com/wreckage

When a van full of young volunteers is hit by a truck, two girls are suddenly connected forever. One holds onto life, wrapped in bandages in the hospital, while the other dies long before her time. Two families struggle, one to hope and the other to grieve. A community of friends, neighbors, and ghosts try to understand. But there is still one truth about the girls that none of them yet knows, and it will bring some of them devastation, and others a miracle in this poetic and powerful ensemble drama.

THE INEXPLICABLE CHAOS
FACTOR OF MIA GREGORY
Emily Hageman

*Mia's friend Liv is visiting her in the hospital. After Mia attempted to take her own life, brilliant mathematician Liv's logical mind has been struggling to come to terms with what happened, especially because they had a terrible fight just before. Here, Mia produces a complicated math book, and **reconnects** with Liv by speaking her own language.*

MIA

I know you love it, so I'm trying to…but, uh…I do not understand it at all. Well, most of it. There's this one chapter that—I mean, I probably have it all wrong, but…I don't know. It's the chapter about chaos theory.

As far as I could understand, it's like—chaos theory is this idea that the little things that happen to us become like—big over time. I guess. And—it got me thinking about how the things that seem big become small—and sometimes, the small things just leap out at you when you don't expect them to.

I don't know, our lives just seem to be a pattern of these tiny connections that create this intricate web of living and sometimes, in that moment, you can only see the fibers of the web, and the fibers hurt so much, and then you step back—and you step back—and…it all makes so much sense. But none at all.

And how you don't—even understand yourself sometimes until later because you do things that you never thought you'd let yourself do.

And in that moment, it hurts so much because you think, if this is who I am right now, then who will I be? Do I even want to find out?

But sometimes there are moments where you can—recognize that something is happening that you'll remember forever.

And suddenly, things don't seem so chaotic anymore—they seem incredibly, unbelievably structured. Like—a thousand little numbers and letters all falling into place with some beautiful, cosmic click. And you just…and you think, I'm so glad I'm here. I'm so glad I'm alive.

Hey, Liv?

Thank you. You're a good friend.

📖 **Discover:** Liv also has a monologue of her own in this play. For more monologues by Emily Hageman, check out *Northview High School Will Shelter You (If We Must)*. Darcy's monologue is also included in this book.

🎤 **Meet** Mia. The playwright introduces Mia in the Cast of Characters as "(16–18): Sweet, sincere, wounded, and deeply complicated."

READ THE PLAY, a one-act drama for 8–20 actors:

yourstagepartners.com/the-inexplicable-chaos-factor-of-mia-gregory

Liv is one of the most brilliant teenage mathematicians in the country, but she does not understand her best (and only) friend Mia. Like, at all. And now, she's doing this stupid play to try to figure it out. An incredibly moving and empowering story about the chaos we create, and the order we can find in it.

8 MINUTES LEFT
e.b. lee

*The world is coming to an end in eight minutes. Watching her unseen children play at a New Jersey playground, Viola **releases** her worries about the past and the future as best she can, to exist in this moment with her kids.*

VIOLA

These kids.

Fearless. They don't know what it means to fall from high. Not really.

> *(Pause.)*

What am I doing? I can't even let them just...*be*. Even now.

> *(Pause.)*

67,000 miles per hour.

This life...if I just, stay still. Like this.

If I just stop.

I can see everything.

The whole world.

> *(She watches them for a long moment.)*

When the nurse placed you both in my arms, I knew. I knew the two of you would always look out for one another, my Yuri, my Yumi. You breathed in unison, you cried in unison. And when you laughed—I was not prepared for the joy it brought me, the way it would lift me up. No matter how hard my day had been, everything bad didn't take up any space in my mind anymore. All there was, was us three.

You two taught me so much. You two made me the person I am. More than just a mother. You opened my world up to the smallest delights. Like this. Having the swings to yourself on a beautiful spring day.

Giving me a heart attack when you scale the fence like these damn squirrels.

I think about all the "you" you could be.

Brave and bold and kind.

You change my world, just by existing.

You make it a little less cruel.

You would have made it a little less cruel for all of us.

    (Beat.)

Guess I won't get to see the "me" I could be, too.

Maybe I'd be more patient, more relaxed, more fun. Become a better version of me.

Maybe I would have learned to stop rushing you both so much—to get to the next karate lesson, to the next soccer practice, to get through homework, to dinner, to bath, to bed, to keep moving on to the next thing.

I was always pushing you ahead, in time, to grow up. Why?

I couldn't fill the blank spaces on the planner fast enough. Every moment of every day.

Keep going.

Fill your life with purpose.

Why couldn't I just have…done this? Felt the sun on my face, pulled you both to me, breathed you in, pressed your cheeks to mine…

    (To her kids, but they don't hear her:)

I'm sorry, my loves. I wish I could have given you more. You deserved so much more.

More time to grow into your lives.

    (Determined, stands up.)

No. I'm not going to do that.

I'll just move a little closer now. I'll stand here, I'll watch.

I want this, right now.

Just so.

Just exactly so.

Without any cruelty, without any lines of pushy parents behind us, without any whining kids in front of us. You'll swing, higher and higher, I'll push you, I'll let the chains twist while you both squeal. Maybe you'll think, "Our mother, she's fun today!"

(She moves closer to them.)

And I'll have to lie to you once more, my loves, I'm very sorry for that.

Discover: This monologue is an excerpt of a longer solo scene. To read the full scene, and discover more monologues from other characters, explore the full script of *8 Minutes Left.* For more monologues by e.b. lee, read *The Other Side of Christmas.*

READ THE PLAY, a full-length dramedy for 7–22 actors:

yourstagepartners.com/ 8-minutes-left

The world is coming to an end at exactly 4:44PM today, and no one has had any time to prepare. *8 Minutes Left* follows the residents of Charlesville, NJ as they navigate their final moments on this Earth—from a couple with a bunker in their backyard who can't quite figure out how to get in, to a mother observing her children on a playground as she wonders what their lives would have become, this thoughtful and keenly observed play manages to find the intimate humor of humans in crisis.

THE CURIOUS CASE OF THE COTTINGLEY FAIRIES
Claire Wittman

*Decades after Lillian took a series of famous photographs that appear to show her cousin Mabel surrounded by fairies, she recalls a note she received from a reporter, claiming to have discovered the truth: it was a hoax. Now, speaking to the reporter's curious granddaughter, Lillian **offers** another way to look at what "the truth" really means here.*

LILLIAN

I wonder. I've wondered for fifty years. Listen:

Just as quickly as our meteoric rise, Mabel and I and our fairy photographs faded into obscurity.

The war ended. Both our fathers survived, by some unknown grace—and Mabel and her mother and father stayed in Cottingley with my parents for the rest of their lives. But I left home.

I travelled the world, with my camera in hand, telling other people's stories rather than my own. The night Josephine Baker first danced in Paris, I was there.

I witnessed the desolation of the Dust Bowl on the American West, and felt my heart break as a second World War destroyed countless lives…in the camps, on the battle-fields, in the Blitz, in Hiroshima. I cheered Queen Elizabeth II at her coronation, and I wept when the Reverend Doctor King received his Nobel Prize.

For I had realized, with time, that there was something to be said for photographing people—if you could help them trust you enough to catch them unguarded. And if you could trust them, too, to show you who they really are. I've seen half a century of perfect truth, whether joyful or tragic, captured on film…and the quality better and better, too.

Meanwhile, Mabel married, had children of her own… and she believed in the fairies till the day she died.

(Lillian shows a photo of herself and an older Mabel, who clearly died far too soon.)

I made it back to Cottingley, for the first time in nearly fifty years, in time to say goodbye. And that, as you may know, was just a month ago, now. Here she is…here we are together.

📖 **Discover** the inspiration behind this play, the fascinating true story of the Cottingley Fairy photographs, which even involved Sir Arthur Conan Doyle and Houdini. What can your research about these historical figures and the photos bring to your performance?

For another historical piece that explores the world of Arthur Conan Doyle, read Claire Wittman's play *Moriarty's Daughters.*

READ THE PLAY, a historical fantasy for 14–21+ actors:

yourstagepartners.com/the-curious-case-of-the-cottingley-fairies

When Lilli Barnes was sixteen years old, she saw a fairy. Encouraged by her impressionable little cousin Mabel, Lilli snaps a photograph, and suddenly, what started as a magical game to distract from the worry of the Great War becomes a national sensation, attracting gullible authors, skeptical reporters, and eccentric spiritualists from all over the world. But swept up in the strangeness of their supernatural sighting, and daunted by the pressures of newfound fame, Lilli and Mabel are left to wonder if they can believe their eyes…or if the "magic" they've uncovered is merely imagination gone wild.

THE VISITORS
Del Martin

Young KB is in a coma for an unknown reason. Here, her older sister Karen arrives in her hospital room to see her for the first time, and **processes** *her feelings about what is happening in real time as she tries to figure out what to say to her unconscious sister.*

KAREN

Hey… Hey, Kiddo, I… I…

> *(Karen retreats to a chair.)*

I don't know what to say. I want to say some sort of big sister, inspirational thing that's going to snap you out of whatever it is that has happened to you. But I'm just lost. I'm tired and I'm lost. I spent all night on a plane. All night with so many questions doing jumping jacks in my head. How did this happen to you? What exactly happened? No one has any answers.

I'm not doing this right. I'm not supposed to come in here and complain. I'm just supposed to tell you that I love you. I love you and I believe you will get better. *(Stands up.)*

And I do believe that. I really do, but right now, I'm just angry. I'm so angry. It's just so random and so wrong. You're KB. You're my little sister. You're just a smart, funny kid who is obsessed with Doctor Who and thinks banana flavored candy is the greatest thing humans have ever invented and who once ate thirty-two Pizza Bagel Bites in an hour. This is not supposed to happen. Not to you.

You know what's infuriating? Being angry and at the same time, not being sure exactly who or what I'm angry at. Who is to blame? I need an object for my hatred and all I have staring back at me is the endless, cold universe. I want to scream. I want to throw things. This shouldn't be happening to you and I need someone to yell at. *(Wipes her brow.)* You'd say, "Then scream. Shout at the stars." And then you'd probably yell something at the sky, just to make me laugh. That's what you'd do.

You always know what to say. You always know how to bring some light into the darker moments in life. That's what you do. I wish I knew how to do that. I wish I could say something right now that would make you laugh…to wake you up.

But I'm not you. I don't have that special spark that makes you, you. So all I can say is, I love you. I believe in you. And when you wake up, I'll be here and we'll laugh together.

📖 **Discover** more Del Martin monologues in his plays *Those Who Remain Turn the Pages, The Hauntings at Cedar Park,* and *In the Forests of the Night.*

🔎 **Meet** Karen. Her entrance may offer insight: "*(Karen enters with a backpack slung over the shoulder. She's a bit out of breath, as if she ran off a plane, hopped in a cab, jumped out and ran to the room. Karen drops the backpack on the floor and approaches the bed, but as she gets closer and looks at KB, she stops.)*"

READ THE PLAY, a one-act drama for 14 actors:

yourstagepartners.com/the-visitors

KB is in a coma. How she got there, no one knows. As she lies unconscious on a hospital bed, family, friends, and other well-wishers reflect on KB and how she has affected their lives. But as KB's physical condition worsens and her visitors struggle with their grief, KB embarks on a mysterious journey that will change her forever.

THE AFTER
Werner Trieschmann

In the immediate aftermath of a shooting at her high school, Shereese expressed feeling disconnected from the tragedy—she was eager to leave high school, and she didn't know any of the seven people who died personally. Six months later, she recalls a long-forgotten memory, and **discovers** *that she is more connected to one of the students who died than she realized.*

SHEREESE

I can't believe it. I had a date with Toby—one of the kids in the seven. I didn't think I knew any of them. I forgot—I don't know how. This was when I was in seventh grade. Me and a bunch of my friends went to the fair and we met up with these boys. One of the boys was Toby. Everybody acted like it was a surprise or something but I think it was a set up. They were all there so they could get us together, me and Toby.

We went off on our own and walked all over the fair. We played the games and saw these rabbits in a cage. He was so quiet—he barely said anything—but he was smiling the whole time. Then we went on the Ferris wheel and it stopped at the top. His friends found us and were yelling up at him, wanting him to kiss me. He just smiled. After that, we walked around some more and it was getting late, the fair was closing.

He reached out and held my hand. Like he was my boyfriend.

But then the fair was over. I don't remember why I didn't see him again after the fair but I didn't. Maybe he had another girlfriend. We were in seventh grade. We were kids.

He died in this school. He was shot in this hallway. I didn't go to his funeral. I didn't...he held my hand at the fair.

📖 **Discover** another monologue from Shereese, as well as several other monologues from female characters, in the full script of *The After.*

✐ **Play** with contrasting monologues to dive into a character's evolution. Shereese's monologue earlier in the play takes place before she realizes her personal connection to Toby. What can you learn about this character as a person by comparing the way she processes the tragedy before and after this revelation? What about her character seems consistent in both monologues? What specific images or moments from that monologue can you bring to your performance of this one?

READ THE PLAY, a full-length drama for 14–30 actors:

yourstagepartners.com/the-after

One bright, blue fall afternoon a shooter walks in Three Roads High School and kills five students and two adults. During the shooting, students in one section of the school put up a makeshift barrier of desks, chairs, music stands— and a photo of the wall goes viral. In the hours, weeks, and months after the wake of another tragedy, students and teachers deal with grief, the media frenzy, and uncomfortable scrutiny that comes along with this horrible violent event that's become all too common in America.

A one-act version of this play is also available.

TRIALS: THE STORY OF JOAN OF ARC (AND BETH)
James DeVita

*Beth's relationship with her dad has been rocky lately, and they struggle to communicate, constantly fighting over everything from the party Beth attended over the weekend to her clothes. When her father says he's done trying to talk to her during their latest clash, Beth **lashes out** in response.*

BETH

Don't blame it on me! You're the one who never talks! You don't talk about anything that matters! It's like you totally ignore everything in the whole world! All you care about is if I graduate or if I'm hanging out with boys or not. You never talk to me about anything important!

Not about what *I* want to talk about! Do you ever think about what the world's going to *be* like when I *do* graduate? You want to know what I was doing that night that you're all so freaked out about, Dad? When I *ran away* to the big *wild party* with the boys? Sorry to disappoint, but we weren't drinking or doing drugs—we were talking. We were talking about how all of us are afraid to go do anything by ourselves anymore. We were talking about whether or not it's safe to go hang at the mall 'cause there's like this "yellow alert" on or whatever. We were talking about whether or not any of us are going to have to die in a war when *we're* eighteen. Or if there's going to be any environment left to breathe in. *(Beat.)* That's what we were doing that night, Dad. So, you want to talk? Talk to me about that.

Yeah, I know, I'm over-reacting, I'm being *dramatic* again—but you know what, Dad? It *is.* It really *is* that dramatic! I wish it wasn't, I wish I could just worry about what to wear, or what weird color to dye my hair, or what boys like me or what girls hate me—but I can't, I can't stop thinking about what horrible thing is happening somewhere in the world right now, and you know what? Every day I'm right, every day something *has* happened. It's not like when you were a kid anymore, Dad. You have no idea!

✗ **Play** with memory. In this outburst from Beth, emotions she has bottled up from past incidents come pouring out. Explore how you can make these memories feel specific so that you can access these emotions.

Through free-writing or improvisation, imagine the get-together where Beth discussed her fears with her peers. Who exactly was there? What kind of a space were they in? What was Beth wearing? How was she sitting? Did she speak, or mostly listen? How did it feel?

You might do the same with a moment with her dad when Beth felt like "All you care about is if I graduate or if I'm hanging out with boys or not."

READ THE PLAY, a full-length historical drama for 7–26 actors:

yourstagepartners.com/trials

Before the myth, there was a girl. Beth's constant clashes with her family make home feel like an emotional battleground. As Beth becomes immersed in a project about Joan of Arc, past and present poignantly intertwine onstage as both conflicted young women face the realities around them—and learn unexpected truths about themselves.

COMEDIC
MONOLOGUES

NO SUBSTITUTES
Don Zolidis

*Vanna is a student in a class that the school is using as a testing ground for new potential substitute teachers. Various wildly unsuitable candidates have been coming and going each day, but on the day Jeepers the clown walks through the door, Vanna refuses to engage with him. Here she **recounts** the horrible reason why. It began with a fateful sixth birthday party…*

VANNA

Let me finish my story, clown.

> *(Vanna goes to a dark place. Perhaps she even stands in a spotlight.)*

It was a princess party. The sun was angry that day. Hot as an oven—I was dressed as Ariel, everyone else was dressed as Belle. The cake was Cinderella's castle—white frosting, topped with a plastic figurine of Cinderella and her prince, their poorly painted little faces frozen in an expression of alarm or joy, no one could tell which.

And then came the clown: Boo Boo. He had his usual clown tricks. Oversize shoes. A buzzer handshake. The squirting flower in the lapel. Behind his white makeup I could see his vacant grey eyes—I loathed Boo Boo on sight.

But we managed. Ariel and seven Belles, sweating and chanting—humoring this dead-eyed clown.

My brother, however, had other designs. He was five years older and had a pet python named Gus—Gus was eight feet long and sweet as a kitten, but my brother loved bringing him out to terrify us.

My brother looped the python in his arms and crept into the party, right behind Boo Boo. And then, as the clown turned, Gus was right in front of him. His clown mouth, painted red like a fire engine, opened in shock, all his little clown tricks firing. Water squirting from his flower as he reached out and grabbed the python.

(It's hard for Vanna to go on.)

The electric shock from the buzzer in his hand, combined with the water…ignited the snake. Smoke shot from Gus's eyeballs… My brother reeled back and flung the sparking python into the air…where he struck the ceiling fan—on its highest setting due to the heat.

Gus…exploded. Flaming chunks of snake, propelled by the ceiling fan, arced into the living room like debris from a mortar shell. Blood rained down upon eight screaming princesses, and I looked with horror—

To the kitchen—where Gus's severed head landed with a plop…on my birthday cake—crushing Cinderella and her prince, setting the trick candles—ablaze.

I heard Boo Boo's faltering voice… "Happy Birthday to you…" as my friends, their yellow dresses now speckled red with snake blood, fled. Two of them broke through a window, another rammed into the front door—one of my friends hurled herself into our large aquarium.

You don't come back from that.

We moved cities. Changed identities. Started a new life. And that's why I do not prefer the company…of clowns.

Discover: Don Zolidis is a prolific playwright with many monologues for female characters in his comedies such as *Haters* and *Princess Party Smackdown*, as well as dramas such as *Monster* and *The Littlefield Gazette Does Not End Today.*

☞ **Unlock** monologues with language. What can the type of language that a character uses tell you about them? For example, in Vanna's monologue from *No Substitutes*, she uses serious, dramatic language (like "the sun was angry that day") to describe completely absurd images ("water squirting from [the clown's] flower as he reached out and grabbed the python"). What can that tell you about who she is?

How can you combine other information you find about the character in the text with their use of language? Can it help you make more specific choices? For example, does Vanna's big vocabulary and detailed language read differently knowing the she's a student than it would if her character were a teacher?

READ THE PLAY, a one-act comedy for 8–25+ actors:

yourstagepartners.com/no-substitutes

It's usually a pretty low-key day when you get a substitute teacher, but not so for Miss Florence's class. The "cool" assistant principal is using them as guinea pigs to try out a series of new prospective subs, from a wannabe inspirational teacher, to a conspiracy theorist, to a border collie. It's almost enough to make you want to quietly finish your work! You never know who's going to show up next in this outrageous comedy full of larger-than-life characters.

ALL THE GIRLS HATE ME AT WEST HADDOCK HIGH
A.M. *Dittman*

When a fellow student desperate for a date approaches Allison to ask her to the dance, Allison passive-aggressively **proposes** *a different type of prom date...for science.*

ALLISON

You know, I think maybe I will go to the dance with you.

(Beat.)

Not, of course, as your date. It won't be a date date. As you know, I'm interested in the human condition. I am prepared to go to the dance with you as a social experiment. I will take notes and then write a paper based on my findings. You will be judged on a scale of one to ten in a variety of different categories. Your score will be tabulated at the end and that's for you to keep. It'll be your number. A number between one and ten. I will judge you on appearance, smell, likability, conversation skills, social graces, dancing ability. Things like that. Everything you say or do will go into my report. Whether or not you try to kiss me, what you wear, how you smell, how sweaty your hands are. Et cetera.

(Beat.)

I don't know if it will be in a scientific journal or just online for everyone to peruse. But it will be made widely available. In the end, it's all about helping humanity.

(Beat.)

You are saying no to me? You are not brave.

📖 **Discover** more plays with monologues by A.M. Dittman, including *Holiday Party* and *Superhero Issues.*

🔑 **Unlock** monologues in the moments the characters *don't* speak. Where might you take a beat, a breath, a pause, or a moment in your performance to set off your words? What is the character thinking in that moment? What shifts? What humor or drama can you find there?

You can start by looking for the pauses written into the monologue's text. Some playwrights may indicate a pause in a stage direction: for example, A.M. Dittman uses "*(Beat.)*" in Allison's monologue from *All the Girls Hate Me at West Haddock High.*

Other pauses might be suggested by the way a playwright structures a monologue. Is the monologue organized in paragraphs? Does a new paragraph begin a new thought? What happens in the character's head in the moment between the end of one thought and the beginning of another?

Don't forget about punctuation, too. For example, in Allison's monologue, look at how A.M. Dittman uses periods. How would the following line read differently if this were all one sentence? What do the periods tell you about where the pauses fall? "Your score will be tabulated at the end and that's for you to keep. It'll be your number. A number between one and ten."

READ THE PLAY, a one-act romantic comedy, 6–22 actors:

yourstagepartners.com/all-the-girls-hate-me-by-a-m-dittman

The one where the boy tries to find a girl who likes him. Always tougher than it sounds. Just ask that guy over there. Or there. Or right there. Or there. And yeah, that guy over there too.

LAST DAY OF SCHOOL
Ian McWethy

*Kassia's been waiting outside the principal's office for a meeting, but her fellow student, the uptight Jared, just marched in and demanded to go in first. When she protests, his petulant response—"I said I was sorry!"—sends her over the edge of patience. Here she **calls out** his behavior.*

KASSIA

No of course you don't understand. You and your preppy expensive shirt and dumb Republican haircut! You think you're always right and everyone else is always wrong. Well guess what, you DID NOT say I'm sorry! You know how I know!?

Because the whole time you're yelling at me I'm thinking "this guy is a big jerk for yelling at me for no reason. But you know what? Maybe he's had a bad day? Maybe I should give him the benefit of the doubt and just wait for him to apologize." And I wait, and I wait, and I wait for you to say you're sorry. And you know what doesn't happen? You know what two words I don't hear? I'm. Sorry. I hear excuses: that you yelling at me wasn't your fault, that you're under pressure. Blah blah blah. And then I hear you say, "well I said I was sorry."

Which I know you didn't say because those are THE ONLY TWO WORDS I WANT TO HEAR! AND YOU DIDN'T SAY IT! OKAY! YOU…stuffed shirt! You didn't say you were sorry!

📖 **Discover:** Ian McWethy's *Last Day of School* includes more monologues for female characters, and flexible characters that can be played as female, too.

🎤 **Meet** Kassia. The playwright describes Kassia in the production notes as "18, badass, alternative, rebellious, cool."

READ THE PLAY, a full-length dramedy for 4–18 actors:

yourstagepartners.com/last-day-of-school

On the final day of classes at Rochester High School, a renegade student takes over the morning announcements and proposes that everyone do something bold. Or unexpected. Or brave. Or stupid. The point is, you may not have another chance, so now's the time to stop being a wallflower and kiss the girl (or guy!). To let your enemies know that you have always hated their guts. Or to do something as simple as climb the rope in gym without throwing up. Through a series of interconnected scenes, misconceptions, grudges, and secret crushes come out into the open in hilarious and surprisingly touching ways. A comedy with a lot of heart, and no regrets.

A one-act version of this play is also available.

There is a version with more female roles available.

KNOCK KNOCK
Kathryn Funkhouser and Jason Pizzarello

Logan's package delivery job has been one battle after another lately, and now her final customer is refusing to accept his order. When he asks her if she thinks she's giving the "one hundred and ten percent" customer service her delivery company promises, she **rebukes** *him with the truth of everything she has put up with on the job.*

LOGAN

You know what? I'm sorry, but the last few weeks I've been giving *two* hundred and ten percent. I got tipped with a toaster. I got signatures from a ghost and my ex. I stopped a robbery! Anybody sane would have walked off the job at any one of those doors. But I saw them all through. The company can say "one hundred and ten percent" as much as they want, but you know what? Maybe *I'm* the one who actually cares about these customers. Because I take pride in getting the job done, even when it's impossible. My friend called HQ when this lady wanted me to knit an entire sweater in one day, and you know what they told him? Figure it out if you want to keep your job. So I knit the sweater, but all the other customers had to wait. If this company really gave two cents about any customer, maybe they would listen to us. *(A sigh.)* So yeah, I'm providing customer service. I delivered every single package on my list today. Except the one you're holding. Please accept the package.

❧ **Note:** This role is listed as flexible, so Logan may be portrayed as a female character or not as the actor or production desires. How will you build your character?

⊷ **Unlock** monologues with tactics: what different means does your character use to try and achive their objective? How do they try to get what they want?

Where exactly in the monologue does your character shift from one tactic to another? Why does your character shift tactics when they do? Do they encounter an obstacle? Does another character push back? Do they lose their nerve?

As an exercise, try placing an object across the room from you or have a scene partner stand in for your objective. As you read the monologue and move across the room toward your objective, try to physically move in a different way every time you switch tactics in the monologue. For example, if your scene partner across the room has a dollar, and the dollar is your objective, and your first tactic is to intimidate them, you might at first move threateningly…then, if you shift to giving them a compliment, you might start dancing toward them charmingly. See what you can discover about creative ways to portray your character's tactics.

READ THE PLAY, a one-act comedy for 4–23 actors:

yourstagepartners.com/knock-knock

When you deliver packages, anyone might be behind your next door, from your elementary school teacher to a burglar on the job. Jaded veteran Logan has seen it all, while newbie Sam is convinced attitude is everything. The only sure thing in this job? They're both going to be surprised. *Knock Knock* is a rapid-fire comedy that delivers.

THE OTHER SIDE OF CHRISTMAS
e.b. lee

When her father twists his ankle, Maude tries to take over his yearly tradition of waiting in line to buy gifts for the family at the Black Friday sale—only to realize she's woefully unprepared in comparison to the more intense shoppers on line with her. Here, she **surrenders** *in the great battle that is Black Friday Christmas shopping.*

MAUDE

Gah, I guess I've done it all wrong? What was I thinking?

I should know better! I should know…something! Right?

I thought you just stand in line and everyone lines up and you get the thing you need. But why would I think that? It's not a *cafeteria!*

It's like I forgot how shopping works!

And *this* is like shopping plus ten times the intensity!

…

…

Black Friday, all of this, this was my Dad's thing you know? He never told me what to do! And I always wanted to go, but he said, *No, you should get some good sleep, it's been a long day. Go play with your brothers. I'll see you in the morning!*

And then on Christmas morning, there was always that one *thing* for Mom, tied up in a humongous bow, you know? One majestic gift that he had really stayed out for like, hours and hours in the dark and cold…and we'd be in awe like, *How did he do it?*

And we'd be screeching like she won the lottery and he'd stand there in the corner, looking so proud. I just wanted to do that once, because he can't. Maybe as a way to say thank you.

...

...

I'm sorry, Dad!

I failed!

I failed at Black Friday!

I thought I could do it!

This is sooooo much more stressful than I thought it would be!

Discover: *The Other Side of Christmas* includes several other monologues, including a great dramatic monologue for the character Eleanore. For more monologues by e.b. lee, read *8 Minutes Left.*

READ THE PLAY, a holiday drama for 8–35+ actors:

yourstagepartners.com/the-other-side-of-christmas

It's easy to look at the Christmas season through rose-colored glasses, but the scrappy radio show "The Other Side" makes it their mission to bring you a different point of view. Through a series of vignettes, host Thomas May guides his audience through moments that aren't exactly holiday card material…some funny, some poignant, all unexpected. *The Other Side of Christmas* is a heartfelt and humorous play about putting down the burdens of perfection and embracing what truly makes the holiday season special—each other.

GAME NIGHT (HUMANS ONLY, PLEASE)
Laura Neill

In an apocalyptic future, the high school nerds who have made the library their base are worried about their friend Avery, who went out for food and never came back. When the soccer team arrives on their doorstep, they're suspicious as they debate whether to let them in. Just as the conflict comes to a head, Avery returns—wearing a soccer jersey. Here, Avery **spills** *the truth to her non-jock friends.*

AVERY

I JOINED THE TEAM.

    (Everyone stares.)

I was never dead and I was never going to break in and get gummy worms from Rite Aid, I wanted to play soccer, okay, I've always wanted to play soccer, I like the grass and the mud and the movement and the adrenaline and the kicking and the shoving and the scoring and the team thing and the passing and the rush and the wind and the sky and the getting out of breath because I'm doing something, and the winning and the losing and the orange slices and the stupid shin guards and the long socks and the dumb jerseys, and back when it existed I liked the audience and the rules and the refs and all those things don't exist anymore, but I still like the cleats and the tendons and the sweat and I like my cleats leaving holes in the actual ground and I like getting dirt all over my sleeve and tearing just enough skin off my leg on a slide to bleed and look amazing but not break any bones but even if I did break a bone I WOULD STILL LIKE IT because I LIKE SOCCER! …And none of you ever understood, you were always making these jokes about how stupid soccer was and how great we were and so I thought well, if I want to fit in I can't join the team, and then the world ended and climate change sunk our town and mutant lizards who can shape-shift into people invaded and Blaze didn't come back so I thought this is my last chance, you know, so when I went scouting a couple weeks ago I didn't go scouting, I didn't actually check the least for scales and tails, I haven't been checking at all the last few weeks because I didn't want everything to just be about the world ending, I went to practice, I went to soccer practice because I love soccer and I play soccer and I joined the team.

🔖 **Note:** The character of Avery uses she/they pronouns.

📖 **Discover** more monologues in Laura Neill's play *Between the Stories.*

READ THE PLAY, a one-act sci-fi dark comedy for 12–24 actors:

yourstagepartners.com/game-night-humans-only-please

It's game night at the end of the world. The library is one of the only places still above the water line, and the nerds are living it up while they can. But when the soccer team shows up because their field went un-derwater, they begin a more dangerous game. A high-stakes dark comedy about mutant lizards, climate change, and being the generation born to watch the water level rise. 

THE CAST LIST
Rocco Natale and Jason Pizzarello

Aspiring actress Lauren is waiting for the director of her school's upcoming production of Romeo and Juliet *to post the cast list. Here, she* **pretends** *to be much more relaxed about casting than she really is.*

LAUREN

I don't want to say that like—Juliet is—like—my dream role, but Juliet is—like—my dream role. Like—if anyone ever asks me—like—who I want to play—I'm totally like: Juliet. Because she's my dream role. Like more than even Maria Von Trapp, which is my other dream role, but no, like Juliet is like—IT. Like, Juliet is like THE dream role. Yeah. It's definitely Juliet and THEN Maria Von Trapp. I also want to play Elphaba some day. When I'm old…like thirty. So, like…those are my top three, but like definitely Juliet is first. Like, Juliet is—like—THE dream role.

Okay you know what? Elphaba and THEN Juliet, and THEN Maria Von Trapp. Because Elphaba is like…epic. Not that Juliet isn't like epic…'cause she totally is—like she has the balcony scene and she dies and stuff, but like—still, Elphaba gets to fly, so like…probably because of the flying, Elphaba is my dream role, but Juliet is my second dream role…THEN Maria Von Trapp. Yeah. Elphaba, Juliet, Maria. In that order. But like…wait what was I saying?

Oh yeah. Okay. Juliet is—like—my DREAM role since we're doing this show and not *Wicked* or *Sound of Music*, so—like—I really want to be Juliet. But my bestie since birth (Jennifer Lucille), I call her JenniLu…JenniLu really wants to be Juliet. And I—like—really really really want that for JenniLu, 'cause I'm like a really really good friend. But I also like really really want to play Juliet myself. And I'm gonna totally be happy for JenniLu if she gets it, she's like I mean like she and I are—like—so close… But I mean at the end of the day… I still really want to play Juliet.

OK… Do you know what… I'm just gonna say something… I don't really think JenniLu would be as good as me. There I said it. That feels so good to get off my chest. Like no shade to JenniLu, I mean she's basically my sister, but she's like a comedic actress and I'm like a serious actress. Like—I've done five plays and she's only done one. Also, I took a zoom acting class from this place in New York last year, and I just feel like I would be a better Juliet.

But if she gets it… I'm gonna like… Of course be happy for her. I'm—like a really nice person, I'm not petty at all, I'm just saying I genuinely in my heart think I would do a better job than she would. But again, she's like my sister, so I feel—like—super bad saying that but… She has lots of dream roles, and I mean this is my dream role. Well like… My second dream role.

Discover more monologues in the full script of *The Cast List.* For more backstage comedies by Jason Pizzarello, read *This Murder Was Staged, Places in Five,* and *When Bad Things Happen to Good Actors.*

READ THE PLAY, a one-act comedy for 10–30 actors:

yourstagepartners.com/ the-cast-list

Ah, the cast list. It would be simple if it weren't for constant script cuts, actor trade agreements, backstabbing, helicopter parents, hysterical prima donnas, and the Assistant Director could figure out how to incorporate the songs of *Grease* into *Romeo & Juliet* without getting sued. This is a show for any student who has ever been cast or miscast in a school play.

HEART OF SNOW
Adam Szymkowicz

*During a long winter in a lakeside community, Kelly writes a letter to Lou to **declare** how she really feels...which turns out to be a little complicated, and has some demands attached.*

KELLY

Dear Lou,

I tremble as I write these words. My breath catches in my throat. I'm terrified because I've never known how you feel about me—not really. But I felt like it was time to tell you how I feel about you.

I hate you. Like I truly and viscerally hate you. Which is a problem because I'm in love with you. I don't know if this will be a surprise to you to hear this from me or if it's really really obvious.

I've tried many times to change how I feel about you but every day it seems it just gets more intense in both directions. So it is you that has to change.

Please try harder not to be so awful. I know that's difficult for you but I also know you can do it. Please try to dress better and be less disgusting more of the time. Please be kinder and quieter and please stay out of my dreams. I think about you enough during the day. Really it's the least you could do.

I'm sending this through the mail. Everyone likes getting mail, don't they? Please write me a letter back detailing the ways you're trying to improve yourself and also please declare your love for me.

Yours,

Kelly

- 📖 **Discover:** Find more great Adam Szymkowicz monologues for female characters in his plays *The Girl Who Cannot Be Hurt* and *When Jack Met Jill.*

- 🔔 **Note:** This role is listed as flexible, so Kelly may be portrayed as a female character or not as the actor or production desires. How will you build your character?

- 🔓 **Unlock** monologues with music. As an exercise, try "scoring" your monologue as if your character were in a film. Play a piece of music underneath as you read it aloud to see what emotions, themes, or rhythms you can tease out in a surprising way. For example, in Kelly's monologue from *Heart of Snow*, how does it affect your performance if you accompany it with an upbeat, romantic pop song like Carly Rae Jepsen's "Call Me Maybe"? Now, how does it change with an ultra-dramatic piece of classical music, like Verdi's "Dies Irae"? What if it switches halfway through? Experiment with pieces of music as different from one another as possible. The effect can be genuinely dramatic or incredibly goofy (especially for a comedy!). Remember, in most performances or auditions, you won't really have a score—but you might discover a new way to approach a moment in your monologue that you can bring back to your performance.

READ THE PLAY, a full-length dramedy for 8–26 actors:

yourstagepartners.com/heart-of-snow

All around Lake Hayward, it's snowing, so over the course of one extraordinary winter, the people in this New England small town turn to each other for warmth. They might find love, friendship, or even just advice on how to make a really good snow fort. But where will they be when spring comes? A series of surprising scenes converges into a playful, and ultimately uplifting dramedy.

ROGUES' GALLERY
Kathryn Funkhouser and Patrick Greene

*The formidable art critic Michaela Carmichael-Michaels has arrived at the gallery to review a sculpture called "Cardboard Boxes" by the artist Godfrey Nameless. It has been totally destroyed by a series of comic misunderstandings and is now just a soggy pile of torn cardboard…but Michaela refuses to hear any explanation. Here, she **critiques** the piece for herself.*

MICHAELA

—Be quiet.

> *(Very slowly, she walks around the boxes.)*

Do you know, Godfrey Nameless, what it is that you have done?

> *(She removes her sunglasses, still staring at the boxes.)*

DO YOU?!!?!

> *(Michaela whips her head around to look at him.)*

You have moved me.

…

Godfrey, I grew up next door to a box factory, and every day my mama, she would say to me and my little sister Lorraine, "Look at the boxes they left out back, child. The boxes that came out squooshed and torn up, that they spilled coffee on during their break. The boxes that'll never hold nothin'. That's the kinda box you're gonna be, child, if you don't get out of this town." "But what about Lorraine, Mama?" I said. She shook her head. "She's not strong, not like you. You gotta be the box big enough to hold all three of us." So I would look through the window at the factory, and swear that one day I'd be a box like that.

They were perfect. They were empty. And now…so am I.

But maybe…maybe the boxes in the back were the most beautiful of all, because they were part of a bigger story. I see that now. Thank you, Godfrey. Thank you.

✤ **Note:** This role is listed as flexible, so Michaela may be portrayed as a female character or not as the actor or production desires. If you prefer, the character may be called Michael. How will you build your character?

READ THE PLAY, a full-length mystery-comedy for 6–35+ actors:

yourstagepartners.com/rogues-gallery

Two hapless security guards must investigate who destroyed the art gallery's prize sculpture—but every suspect caused mayhem that day, from would-be art thieves and confused tourists, to fumbling custodians and fiendish pranksters. Whodunnit? The better question is, who didn't? And can the guards come up with a really good excuse before the artist comes back? This hilarious build-your-own mystery play can be performed with any combination of components and optional interludes.

This full-length play includes short plays by nine playwrights, each of which may be performed and licensed as individual plays, or as part of the complete full-length play.

IDENTITY PLAY; OR WHO YOU ARE IF YOU THINK YOU ARE
Jason Pizzarello and Jon Jory

*In a job interview, JJ must **justify** a snarky answer she gave to a question on the application…and accidentally heightens it into a philosophical epiphany.*

JJ

So how do I answer the question—shoot now I forgot the question—ummmno, no, I got it: "Name an experience that changed your life." Bam! So to review—or frame, or state, or something: my problem is my life has never been changed. Which is bad news, right? At least in terms of having any extra cash this year.

So what did I write down on the application in the big space after "What experience has changed your life"? I wrote…birth. Just that. Because that's by far the biggest thing that has changed me so far. And get this, they didn't buy it. Frankly, I think too much was expected of me.

   (Beat.)

I'd like to change my answer. To the question: "Name an experience that changed your life," even though I think it's kinda deep and maybe even intrusive to ask that on a part-time job application at a fast food restaurant. A management position maybe I could understand, not for literally flipping burgers.

But I realize my answer about the only life changing event was "being born" was a little…snarky. I didn't mean it that way. Really.

I just meant it was significant. Being born. Obviously. Everyone is born, that's true. So is it significant? I think, yes, it is. Of course it is. It's a miracle, that's why they call it the "miracle of life." Something out of nothing.

But being born is a gift, and maybe sometimes we curse being alive when things aren't going well—or the way we expected—it should still be recognized as a gift. So while being born might not have been an experience that changed my life, realizing that being born is significant changed my life. I've been up thinking about this, and maybe I didn't sleep last night at all and maybe running on fumes has something to do with my revelation—but I'm just feeling extremely humbled to be alive at this present moment.

How does that make me a better applicant? I don't know. I'm grateful for the opportunity. I don't want to waste it. Which is maybe not something I could have always said about myself.

How does this realization about myself change who I am? I don't know. To be honest, I haven't become who I think I am yet. I'm still not there. But I'm on my way. I'm becoming me. I'm a project still in development. It could be said, by wiser folks than me that…that I'm almost born. So stay tuned.

That's all.

Thanks for your consideration.

(Beat.)

I didn't really want to work at Burgersmash anyway.

🍴 **Note:** This role is listed as flexible, so JJ may be portrayed as a female character or not as the actor or production desires. How will you build your character?

📖 **Discover:** This monologue is the first half of a longer monologue that bookends *Identity Play*. Read the full script to discover the full arc of the monologue.

✎ **Play** with the comedic use of tangents in JJ's monologue. We often talk about characters pursuing their objectives, but what happens when they lose track of it? Where does JJ's train of thought go off the rails?

In the text, you might try putting brackets around each time JJ strays from her point. For example, in the first paragraph, you might put brackets around "—shoot now I forgot the question—ummmno, no, I got it:" and "So to review—or frame, or state, or something."

In the rehearsal room, try physicalizing the tangents. Read through the monologue, walking across the room in a straight line when JJ remains on task…and swerving off to the side when she goes on a tangent.

Do the swerves get wilder or longer as the monologue goes on? How might she feel about being waylaid from her objective? Does she get more desperate, or more confident? And in the end, does her objective change?

READ THE PLAY, a one-act dramedy for 10–30+ actors:

yourstagepartners.com/identity-play

A series of comedic and dramatic vignettes exploring who we are and who we want to be. With endless choices and expectations, do our actions define us or do our intentions? What about our words? What about the way we dress, the friends we keep, or how we act online? Is who we think we are different than how other people see us? In such a complex, fast-paced world, it's vital to slow down, reflect…and laugh. 

TOO MANY DETECTIVES AT
THE MURDER MANSION
Ian McWethy

*At a meeting of famous detectives, angsty Batman has just apologized to Miss Marple for gobbling food in a Cookie Monster–esque fashion in front of her. Others usually find it unsettling—but the unassuming Miss Marple **reminisces** about the memory he has awakened with surprising passion.*

MISS MARPLE

Oh, it's quite all right. Honestly, it's kind of refreshing. You remind me of a boy I used to date. This was during the war, many, many years ago. I was a nurse stationed in Paris. He was an infantrymen, who got sent to my ward thanks to a nasty piece of shrapnel lodged in his head. They eventually got most of the shrapnel out, but the bits that remained, well…it made that poor boy eat like…well like you just did. Like a sick animal. And while it disgusted the rest of the nurses in my unit, I found it…strangely exhilarating. It was as if the animal part of my brain had been unleashed and I found myself drawn to this shrapnel boy. And he to me. And for the rest of the war…we were inseparable. I've never had such chemistry with another person. Pure, uncut, chemistry. I'm talking beakers and bunsen burners and foggy smoke. And carbon. So much carbon.

> *(Miss Marple takes a moment to relive those days of her youth, then goes back to her knitting.)*

But I'm sure I'm just an old lady prattling on about a war most people don't care about anymore. I'm sorry. You just reminded me of him, that's all. What was his name? Dewey? Dreary? No! Doorknob. Doorknob McFeeley. At least that's what he said his name was. Hard to know for sure on account of the metal in his brain but…that's what he told me.

✎ **Play** with the many faces of Miss Marple. From the original stories by Agatha Christie to the many adaptations and riffs on the character, Miss Marple has appeared in many forms—but never quite like this. What can you bring from other depictions to this character? What about this Marple is unique? How can you have fun with a "serious" character in a comedic setting?

📖 **Discover** more plays by Ian McWethy that include monologues, like *Last Day of School, Win or Lose, Mascots,* and *I, Chorus.*

READ THE PLAY, a full-length mystery-comedy for 10–20 actors:

yourstagepartners.com/too-many-detectives-at-the-murder-mansion-full-length

Sure, you think you've seen this type of murder mystery before. A cast of eccentric characters meet at a mansion, only to become suspects of a murder that a singular genius detective will eventually solve. But what happens when all the suspects are the detectives? Sherlock Holmes, Nancy Drew, Miss Marple, and Batman are just a few of the guests. *Too Many Detectives at the Murder Mansion* is a whodunnit that will leave you laughing and guessing right until the very end—and there are three different endings to choose from!

A one-act version of this play is also available.

THE DEAD QUEEN REQUESTS THE HONOR OF YOUR PRESENCE AT DINNER
Leah Barker

In conversation with the Dead Queen and the Creature, Leonora has just confessed that she feels guilty for taking the opportunity to escape from France to safety in Spain, while her husband is in a prison camp. She has no way to help him, but is she abandoning him? The Creature is happy to **advise** *her from experience.*

CREATURE

That's sort of like a situation I was in once.

A situation with my ex.

I knew some distance had grown between us because the only thing we could talk about was cicadas.

It was a summer they were coming out of the ground, one of those summers that happens every seven years when the cicadas appear in the trees and sing. And at first we were both fascinated by the cicadas and had some earnest conversations about them, about how big they are, and how loud, and how tasty for the occasional afternoon snack. But then it became this crutch, like whenever we'd run out of things to talk about I'd just say, "Have you seen any cicadas lately?" and we'd have a half-hearted conversation about them. And then it was happening more and more, these awful pauses where we'd stare each other down, smiling politely, and I had nothing to say so I would just say "cicada"!!

Soon I decided I needed to track how many silences and thus how many cicada conversations were happening. So every time I turned to him and said, "I saw a cicada on the tree near the crag," or, "Did you hear that loud cicada this morning?" I would go catch a cicada and put it in a jar.

And then one day I looked in the jar and thought,

> *(Meaningfully:)*

"That is just too many cicadas."

So you see, it happens to everyone.

> *(The Creature smiles as if she's said something very helpful.)*

📖 **Discover:** The *Tenish: Horror* short play collection includes several more great monologues for female characters such as Juniper in *Mirror* and the Narrator in *Transfer.*

This play is loosely based on the life of Leonora Carrington and her painting *The Dead Queens of Cockerham.* What can you bring to this piece from your research on the art and the artist?

READ THE PLAY, a 10-minute horror play for 3 actors:

yourstagepartners.com/the-dead-queen-requests-the-honor

In a clearing deep in a forest, the Dead Queen sits at a magnificent dining table. As her servant puts the final shine on the glassware, they await the evening's guest.

This play is part of the short play collection Ten(ish): Horror.

MASCOTS
Ian McWethy and Carrie McCrossen

Principal Gurgins has just announced that the old school mascot will be replaced, and the assembly has broken out into pandemonium. Now she tries to **convince** *the students that they will have power in choosing a replacement... and convince herself that this is a good idea.*

PRINCIPAL GURGINS

Okay! Okay. Look! I hear you. And I understand that this will be a tough transition for some of you. Change is always hard. But let's remember how important this decision is. I mean we're talking about our school's mascot here, people! Which is a symbol for everything we do and everything we are! I truly believe that a mascot is more than just an over-caffeinated weirdo in a silly costume. The mascot is the soul of a school. Which is why I believe that you, the student body, should decide what our new mascot would be. Now a lot of people told me this was a bad idea. Leaving such an important decision up to the student body. My mother, in particular said I was a "fool" and "needed to get my head out of my you-know-what." But today we're all going to prove my mother wrong! She doesn't own me! Or us. Or...

> *(Principal takes a deep breath. Everyone in the auditorium is like "Yikes, what's going on with her and her mom?")*

Sorry. My mother has been living with me for the last six months. Ever since she got kicked out of her retirement home for excessive swearing and...gambling. It...hasn't been easy. *(One more breath.)* Anyway, the point is I believe in this school! I believe in it more than any hurtful words my mother says. So, without further ado, let's get to it. Let's see the candidates for our new high school mascot, designed and submitted by you, the students!

✦ **Note:** This role is listed as flexible, so Principal Gurgins may be portrayed as a female character or not, as the actor or production desires. How will you build your character?

✦ **Unlock** monologues by shaking up your rehearsals vocally. Though repetition is key to preparing your piece, you also want to make sure it doesn't start to feel like stale recitation. Stay loose by practicing the monologue in a way you might not ever perform it. Try speaking it at twice the speed that you normally would, then again at half the speed. Try it in a whisper all the way through, then run it again in a bellow. Run it once hitting all the consonants in each word twice as hard as usual, then again, emphasizing the vowels. It's probably going to be a bit silly—and that alone can be great to keep your mind engaged with the words! But you also might notice a new moment in the monologue where a change in volume, speed, or emphasis is exciting and effective, too.

READ THE PLAY, a one-act comedy for 6–18 actors:

yourstagepartners.com/mascots

Drysdale High School has a problem. For the first time in their fifty-year history, they need to replace their beloved (but also deeply problematic) school mascot, Cujo. So Principal Gurgins turns to the student body to submit and select a new mascot, one that can represent (and fire up!) Drysdale for the next fifty years. During the play, we'll see new mascots ranging from an ordinary house cat, to the Titanic, to the mineral quartz, to even a bland, inexplicable teal square. A playful comedy that explores something we all cheer for even though we're also scared of them: a mascot.

About the Authors

Visit www.yourstagepartners.com/authors to find each playwright's Stage Partners profile page. There you will find the playwright's full bio and links to each of their scripts in the Stage Partners catalogue. All scripts in the Stage Partners catalogue are available to read online in full.

About Stage Partners

Stage Partners is an independent play publisher dedicated to making exceptional plays accessible to all theatres and schools. Founded in 2015 by two playwrights with extensive backgrounds in theatrical publishing and licensing, Stage Partners was created with the simple idea that regardless of whether you are a new drama teacher or an experienced artistic director, finding the perfect new play should be easy, engaging, and exciting. With scripts that are always free to read, lightning-fast licensing, production & educational resources, and a passionate staff, Stage Partners is committed to offering industry-best services to both its customers and its playwrights. If you are looking for a publishing partner that understands that making theatre happen is hard work, but discovering a great new play should be a breeze, join us at www.yourstagepartners.com and we'll begin together.